KNOW.
LIKE.
TRUST.

Greg Jones is an accomplished entrepreneur and gifted speaker. He speaks on a variety of business subjects, primarily innovative marketing systems and business growth strategies.

Greg can be reached at:
velocitychainreaction@gmail.com

KNOW.

LIKE.

TRUST.

**The Explosive Marketing Sequence
That Can Double The Profitability
Of Your Business
In 6 Months Or Less**

Greg V. Jones

ISBN-13: 978-1523216079
ISBN-10: 1523216077

Printed in the United States of America

Book interior design by Jean Boles
jean.bolesbooks@gmail.com

Book cover design by Dalton Smith
dparks.smith@gmail.com

CONTENTS

PREFACE

*A Preparation Guide for Entrepreneurs
and Small Business Owners*

My name is Greg Jones, and I am writing this book to my favorite "tribe" of people: entrepreneurs/small business owners. Your tenacity, creativity and risk-taking spirit is the energy that makes the world of commerce spin on its axis.

The sparks that fly and the lights that go on when entrepreneurs get together is incredible. I love it.

I am also a marketing expert to small and medium sized-businesses. The proven *marketing system* I will be sharing in this book can totally transform your business/practice and make you dominant in your industry.

This system is the single most powerful catalyst behind the rapid growth and tremendous profitability I experienced with each of my multi-million dollar businesses:

- Business #1 Rocketed from zero to $2.7 million in 9 months.

- Business #2 Grew from a single person operation to having 63 licensees in the US and 3 foreign countries.

- Business #3 A company that I founded around a patented process I developed and was awarded trademark licensing agreements with GM, Ford and Chrysler. With my proprietary process, I was able to develop a "back-end" sales generator that resulted in $1.8 million in sales within 18 mos.

- Business #4 Is a business I co-founded with my son-in-law, creating and producing consumer snack products. We had our products on the shelves of Costco and Walmart within 18 mos. of start-up—virtually unheard of. Sam's Club was added shortly thereafter. By year three the company was generating over $20 million per year in sales. We sold the company in less than 5 years for a very substantial payday.

The products and services of each business were truly outstanding. They had to be in order to compete in the marketplace. And, like any business, we had to learn the ways to outmaneuver our competition.

Yet, in spite of the growing pains, obstacles and hurdles, very <u>specific</u> and <u>strategic</u> marketing systems were the key to the *rapid growth* and *remarkable profits* each of the businesses experienced.

Believe me, innovative marketing is the indispensable key that makes the cash register ring.

David Ogilvy, the Father of Advertising agrees,

"In the modern world of business, it is useless to be a creative, original thinker unless you can also sell what you create."

All things being equal in business—great product, great service, great prospects—the ONE thing that is the great "unequalizer" is masterful marketing— or lack thereof.

Marketing is the ONLY way you can differentiate yourself from your competitors in the long run.

That's why I have written this book detailing certain aspects of the **Velocity Marketing System**, aka **The Know, Like, Trust Sequence**.

This book is a "preparation guide" that will help you to see yourself, your business, your clients and your company's marketing from an entirely new mindset. Prepare to take notes and then prepare to take action.

I love this quote from legendary football coach, Bear Bryant:

> *"It's not the will to win that matters—everyone has that. It's the will to prepare to win that matters."*
>
> **– Paul "Bear" Bryant**

This book is an easy read. It's rather short. And I am only able to share a small fraction of the entire Velocity Marketing System that I utilize when working with businesses and professional practices.

But, honestly, if you implement just 10-20% of the marketing strategies I lay out in the next few chapters, your business or practice will begin to trigger a chain reaction—an explosion—of new clients, increased profitability and competitive advantage in your sphere of business.

INTRODUCTION

To be successful you must know
that the business you are really in
is the Marketing business.

If someone could wave a magic wand and suddenly change something about your chosen profession or business, what one thing would you have them change?

Would you have them provide you with an easier way to contact more, better-qualified prospects? And would you want those prospects, as well as your current customers, to view you as the go-to expert in your field?

You may be good now, but how would you like to be even better at making more effective, more persuasive presentations? Perhaps you would like to be more effective at closing sales or handling objections, or perhaps repeat business more important to you?

What if your current customers felt that you were the only source who understood and could effectively serve their specialized, unique and individual needs?

Or, how about referrals? Take the best customer you have right now. How would you like to have more clients just like them than you could possibly handle? What one thing would you change to make you a better, happier, and more productive businessperson?

In the chapters to follow, we'll be discussing not only these areas, but other factors that are critical for you to realize real business success. Throughout the pages of this guide we'll explore some of the most effective ideas and field-proven strategies and tactics that you can begin to put to use immediately to help you increase your sales, improve your business, overcome some of your most difficult challenges, gain extra income, have more free time, and find a renewed enjoyment from your chosen business.

Increasing Your Effectiveness

You and I both know that it's no secret that things are changing today, faster than ever before.

Technology has become more sophisticated, competition more keen, and consumers have become more educated and aware.

And with the wide variety of choices your customers or clients have, not only in similar products and services from different companies, but also in the individual people they deal with, it stands to reason that the more skillful and professional you are at meeting your customer's needs, the bigger advantage you can command, and the more effective and successful you can become.

If you're really going to be effective and successful in the marketplace today, it is necessary, even vital, that you continually improve your selling, service, and problem-solving skills, as well as your methods of marketing and general business operation. It has been said, and you've no doubt heard, that:

> *"People don't care how much you know,*
> *until they know how much you care."*

One of the best and most effective ways you can show your prospects and customers you care, is by helping them solve their problems in an efficient, cost-effective, and professional manner.

Exposure to New Ideas

And that's what this program is all about. It has been written with the goal of helping you become the best you can be at what you do professionally.

Naturally, this program doesn't claim, nor does it pretend to have all the answers to all your business problems. No book, course or seminar could do that.

Rather, the objective of this program is to expose you to some tried and tested ideas, concepts, and techniques that have worked for other businesses much like yours.

Once acquainted with new information it will then be up to you to decide which ideas can best be tailored to your own individual business needs, and how you will begin to use them to better serve your customers and prospects.

The goal of this program is not to try to make you a marketing guru, but rather, to provide you with some of the tools the experts and those already successful in business are currently using.

Together, we'll explore specific marketing, sales, customer service, and business building techniques that others have used to significantly increase their businesses and incomes, with very little extra effort.

You will most likely find that many of these ideas will be easy to implement, and you'll be able to begin using them right away. Others may take a little longer to gear up for, and still others may not be right for you or your operation at all. That's okay. Every business is unique, and "one size fits all" solutions rarely work.

But if you get just one or two good ideas that you can put into your business operation that make a difference, then your time, effort and money will be well invested.

How We Retain Information

Getting a new idea is one thing, but what you do with it once you have it, is just as important as getting it in the first place. Studies on retention show that you remember:

- 10% of what you read,
- 22% of what you hear,
- 37% of what you see,
- 56% of what you see and hear, and up to
- 86% of what you see, hear and do.

So an idea that is heard but not acted upon is only half as likely to be retained as an idea that is actually put into practice. With that concept in mind then, it is important to understand that if the information presented in this book is to be of any real value to you, it must not only be read, it must be applied. That is to say, it must be experienced, or acted on. And that means it's going to take some effort on your part.

In their book, **The Knowing-Doing Gap,** authors, Jeffrey Pheffer and Robert L. Sutton mention that every year there are 1,700 new business books published, $60 billion spent on training, $43 billion spent on consultants, and our universities turn out 80,000 graduates with MBA's. Yet, most businesses continue to operate in much the same ways as they've always done.

You see, knowledge without action is no better than no knowledge at all. Just knowing isn't enough. You've got to do something with what you to know.

The ideas presented in this manual work. They're not theory. They're not speculation on what "should" work, and they're not philosophical musings. These ideas, concepts and techniques are currently in use by business owners across the country in one form or another. They're being proven in actual field use day in and day out.

They work for others, and they can work for you. But, you're going to have to take the time to study them, understand them and make the necessary modifications to tailor them to your own personal and business style and operation. And then finally, you're going to have to apply them in your business.

Five Steps of Learning and Retention

Learning—the acquisition of new information or knowledge, and Retention—the ability to capture that information and recall it when wanted or needed, is actually a process that involves five steps:

First, is **Impact.** That is, actually receiving the idea in your mind. Impact can be in the form of a word, a visual observation or a concept. It makes no difference. Your mind isn't capable of making a distinction between something you visualize and an actual experience. Nor is it capable of determining the difference between a conscious or unconscious impact an idea may have on you. As far as your mind is concerned, those experiences are all the same and your mind will accept them as fact.

If information or an experience appears real to your mind your emotions and nervous system will react as though it were actually real.

To illustrate this point, try this simple experiment:

Get seated in a comfortable chair, feet flat on the floor and your hands resting comfortably in your lap.

Close your eyes, take a deep breath, let it out slowly and relax.

Take another one. Let it out slowly, relaxing even more.

Picture in your mind a lemon resting on a table in front of you. Visualize it. See it clearly. Look at its shape—its color—its texture.

Now, mentally reach out with your hand and pick up the lemon. Bring it up to your face. Look at it closely. Squeeze it. Do you notice how firm it feels? Feel the texture of the lemon's dimply, waxy skin. Notice the lemon's yellow color and round shape, with its pointy ends.

Now, hold it up to your nose. Smell it. Do you notice the lemon's citrusy smell?

Place the lemon on the table and mentally pick up a knife that's lying nearby. Cut the lemon in two.

Pick up one half of the lemon and see the juice dripping from it. Bring the lemon up to your nose. Smell it again. Now bite into the lemon.

What's happening to you right now? Is saliva flooding your mouth, both in your mind, as well as physically?

Now consider what just happened. In actuality, there was no lemon. You just pictured one in your mind. While this was just a mental exercise, and the lemon was just imagined, chances are, if you are like most people, the mental image you were playing on the screen of your mind triggered certain responses which manifested themselves physically. So, you can see by this demonstration, that *Impact*, is a critical step involved in the process of learning and retention.

The second step is **Repetition.** One university study revealed that an idea that was read or heard only one time was 66% forgotten within 24 hours. But if that same idea was read or heard repeatedly for 8 days, up to 90% of it could be retained at the end of the eight days.

So once you've read this manual all the way through, go back and read it again. But this time read with a highlighter, a pencil and notepad handy. Mark up the book. Write down the ideas you feel fit your personal business situation. This repetition will help you retain more of the information than if you had read it only once.

The third step in the learning and retention process is **Utilization.** This is the "doing" step. It is here that neuromuscular pathways are actually developed, creating "mind-muscle memory." Remember, according to the study quoted earlier, once you physically experience an action, it becomes twice as easy to recall.

The fourth step is **Internalization.** Actually making the idea a part of you. That may involve some customizing or tailoring of the idea to fit your situation or style, but it is vitally important for you to personalize the idea and make it yours.

The fifth step is **Reinforcement.** In order to maximize the effectiveness of an idea, you should continually be looking for ways to support and strengthen it. The more you can support the idea the more you will believe it, the longer you will retain it, and the more effective it will become in helping you serve your customers' needs.

What does all this have to do with your business? In your daily business and personal activities, as well as throughout your experience with the information presented in this book, you are going to be exposed to a great number of ideas.

Some will be brand new, some will be ideas you have heard in the past but have forgotten, and others will be ideas you come up with on your own as a result of something that was triggered in your mind as you read. Understanding and applying these five steps in the learning and retention process can help you maintain more of what you read and experience.

Action Makes the Difference

It's important to keep an open mind as you read, hear, or otherwise experience ideas that can help you. Try not to judge them or cast them aside too quickly because they don't sound good, they're not part of your personality, or because you may have heard them before.

Instead, consider these courses of actions:

If you've heard an idea before, say to yourself, "Yes, I've heard that before, but am I using it?" If not, "Why not?"

If you are currently using the idea, ask yourself, "How effective am I at using it? How can I improve on it to make it even more effective for me and my business?"

Next, ask yourself this question: "What will I do as a result of what I've learned?"

Remember, it's not *what* you know—it's what you *do* that counts. Ideas are powerful. And good ideas are really important for any business. They're what keep your interest up and your business fresh, alive and growing. When they are put into action, good ideas can make a huge difference in the way you do business, the results you realize, the fun you have, and the profits you make.

This book is full of good, practical, and usable ideas that can help make that big difference for you. But it's up to you to tailor them to your own unique situation, and more importantly, to put them into action.

The Business You're in

If you don't learn another thing from our time together, remember this...

You're NOT in the (Whatever business you're in) business...

You're in the *MARKETING* business.

Read those sentences again...and again...and again. Digest them. Understand them. Internalize them. Make them an integral part of your business philosophy. Because unless and until you do, your business will be no better and no different than any of the other choices your prospects and customers can select to do business with.

Let me explain by using the insurance profession as an example, and as I do, think about how these principles might apply to your business.

It's a well-known fact that very few people (if any at all), want to actually buy an insurance policy. It's true, they may want the benefits, security and peace of mind that insurance provides, but they don't necessarily want to spend their money on an insurance policy. That said, what do most insurance sales people sell?

They sell insurance!

It doesn't take a Harvard degree to figure out that if you sell insurance... and know that people don't want to buy insurance... why would you continue to beat your head against the wall trying to sell it?

Consider the way most people shop for auto insurance. They go online and ask for a quote. The agent or his or her representative asks what coverage the caller is currently carrying, and gives a quote based on those figures.

They keep repeating that scenario until they're convinced that they've found the lowest price…and whichever company comes in lowest gets the business.

But, wait a minute. Isn't there more to buying insurance than just "low price?" Well, sure there is, and you and I both know it. So do most insurance agents.

Why is it, then, that nearly every agent from nearly every insurance company you reach out to tries to sell on price, knowing that there's probably someone out there with a lower price than they can quote?

Why is it that so few agents try to differentiate themselves from their competition, and change the prospect's base of thinking away from price, and on to other, more important things?

Price is important, don't get me wrong. It's very important, and it carries a lot of weight in a prospect's buying decision.

But it's only one of many factors that a person needs to consider when making their buying decision.

In actuality, there's very little difference in insurance policies issued by any number of insurance companies in the same geographical area.

And likewise, there's usually very little difference in the products or services you sell versus those same types of products or services sold by your competitors.

General overhead costs, utilities, phones, supplies, wages, and product costs are also similar for most companies that sell like products and services.

So, if all those factors - similarity of products and services, overhead costs and product costs - are pretty much the same, the prices charged by each individual business must, out of necessity, be pretty close, as well.

It's true that one company may, for example, obtain a lower purchase price on their products and as a result, be able to offer a more attractive sales price for a certain period of time, but eventually, things change and the playing field becomes level once again.

There are other factors not to be overlooked such as investment income and tax write-offs or advantages that can play a role in the prices businesses charge for the things they sell.

But all things considered, the prices charged for the goods and services from one company to another similar company are going to be fairly close over the long haul.

The point is, no matter what business you're in...

Long-term you will never be able to maintain a competitive advantage because of the products you offer, or the prices you charge.

As soon as you develop a new product, or offer a new service, it's just a matter of time before your competition latches on to it and offers the exact same thing, or better, at a lower price.

The marketplace you operate in is so fiercely competitive, so cutthroat, so unforgiving that you absolutely *must* do something to differentiate yourself from your competition.

If you don't, you'll be relegated to just another "me-too" business, just like all your competitors.

Just look around. They're all the same, their businesses all look the same, their products are all the same, they walk and talk the same, and their advertising all looks like and says the same things as the next guy's. And because they all operate that way and don't know how to change it gives you a tremendous opportunity!

You see, if they keep on doing what they've always done they'll keep on getting what they've always got.

But you... if you want to get something different you've got to be willing to make some changes. And that's what this program is all about. Making real changes that will produce measurable results in your business.

But, what you'll learn here isn't enough. These ideas and strategies alone won't work. You've got to take action on them if you expect anything different than what you're currently getting.

So, make the action commitment now, and let's get started!

1

Benefits and Hassles:

The Marketing Power Twins

In order to grow, businesses MUST have a marketing *system* in place that can motivate, influence and persuade prospects. "Image" or "institutional" advertising fails miserably in that regard. By "image" marketing I'm referring to ads that primarily promote the brand or name of a particular company as a way of, hopefully, winning favor with the buying public.

But, who cares if you've "been in business 45 years" and you "claim" to have the best customer service in the galaxy. Everyone else's advertising

31

says the same things about their businesses. Image advertising is really egocentric, rather than taking a customer-centered approach.

Marketing that is going to be genuinely effective must be directed, first and foremost, from an understanding of what a customer wants at an emotional, "gut level."

And that emotional connection is most typically determined by discovering the *benefits* a customer is wanting to experience from your product or service or the *hassle* a prospect believes your product or service will remove from their lives (which is actually a benefit as well).

Every smart business marketing system must be based upon those two factors: "What benefit can my product/service provide my customer? What hassle does my product/service remove for my customer?

Here's an example: You most likely have seen the Planet Fitness ads that depict a sweet soccer mom in her 30's making her first visit to a fitness "gym" (we'll call her "Jill").

The place is dimly lit and filled with muscular, sweaty, tattooed, weight-lifter types. Jill is looking around, very stressed and confused and feeling out of place when she timidly asks the question,

"Can't we just roll around on my yoga ball?"

The next scene opens with Jill standing in a nicely appointed, well-lit room in front of a smiling, friendly female manager. She looks at Jill and says reassuringly, *"Don't worry. There's no 'gym-timidation' here at Planet Fitness."*

The Planet Fitness ad is genius because it addresses the most important, gut-level, *hidden* fear (hassle) in Jill's mind concerning fitness centers: Jill's overwhelming feelings of *intimidation* (hassle) and her desire to feel *secure.* (benefit)

Wow. Absolute marketing genius. Let's just break it down a bit and see why Planet Fitness' marketing system is so successful:

1) Most fitness centers **assume** that the #1 "benefit" desired by a 25-40 year-old soccer mom is to "lose weight." But studies showed that a woman's *fear of intimidation* is even greater than their desire for weight loss. But 95% all fitness centers overlook the real benefit their female prospects are seeking.

2) Therefore, most fitness centers advertise by showing off their high tech, modern equipment designed to help folks get in shape. Those items are "features" not "benefits."

3) Or, they brag about how many stores they have around the country. And, they'll usually show images of super-fit, model-caliber "clients" in the hopes of convincing the prospect that, they too, can look the same way if they will just come and sign up.

The (image) ads all essentially say:

"Look at how great WE are."

"Look how advanced OUR equipment is." "Look at the kind of people WE attract."

Nothing but ego-centric, "image" advertising that virtually EVERY business uses because they have been convinced the purpose of marketing is to "keep our name out there" or, "build our brand."

Really????

Because all of the "Jills" in your market could care less that you have 1,000 fitness centers across the nation.

And, Jill is not interested in how massive your "free weight" area might be.

And, Jill most certainly isn't attracted to a fitness center that has mostly buff guys and gals with perfect figures exercising next to her!

Those are the very reasons Jill is feeling intimidated in the first place!

Jill's desire to lose the intimidation is greater than her desire to lose weight by joining a "gym"!

Look, Planet Fitness understood Jill's concerns (Know), affirmed that Jill was normal for feeling that way (Like), then assured Jill that Planet Fitness had "removed" Jill's greatest fear about fitness centers so that Jill could enjoy herself without feeling intimidated (Trust).

Know. Like. Trust. ...

Wins the marketing battle every time. Because focusing on the "benefit" to the customer, rather than on how "great" the company is makes the customer feel they are understood and they are valued.

It's important to make this point again:

The genius behind Planet Fitness' marketing is that they drilled down to the bottom of the real issue facing their prospective clients, the MOST IMPORTANT reality in their prospective client's mind and emotions concerning "working out"—the fear of intimidation.

"I feel so intimidated just to go in the door of a fitness center where everyone else might look at me with disgust because I'm twenty pounds overweight!"

Or, "I feel so intimidated because I don't know the first thing about how to adjust and operate the training equipment."

"I'm so intimidated about looking stupid and out of place!"

You see, when your business uses a marketing system that makes a science out of understanding the "Jills" of your market, your competition won't have a prayer.

Why? Because you will have set in motion a chain reaction that *will* create—for your company—a superior advantage in motivating, influencing and persuading prospects to become your clients.

Clients that will gladly buy your products and services. Clients that appreciate that your business truly takes the time to discover the benefits they *really* want from your product or service.

Someone astutely observed,

> *"The best marketing is to go into the mind of your prospect and enter into the conversation they are already having about your product or service."*

Every business owner ought to chew on that one for a while. That's marketing mindset *gold*.

It's impossible to over-emphasize the value of having a marketing system that is based upon digging deep and "entering the conversation" in your prospect or client's mind to discover what they really want—on an emotional level. The emotions of your client are what drive them to buy.

Here is a good exercise for any business owner:

Take out a piece of paper and "become" your client. Put yourself into their mindset by putting yourself in their shoes:

"What are they most concerned/nervous about when purchasing a product/service like mine."

"What benefit are they most wanting from my product or service?"

"What areas do they most feel ignorant about regarding my product or service, that could make them feel intimidated about discussing it?"

"What can I do to educate them better about my product or service so that we can have a helpful, productive conversation about my client's needs rather than me just trying to "sell" my service/product to them?

That's why marketing should be all about—and ONLY about—what I call, the **Know, Like, Trust** Sequence.

When prospects get to know you and really believe that you "**know**" them—that you truly "get" them—a relational sales chain reaction is triggered.

They begin to "**like**" you because a congenial, helpful and beneficial relationship has started to develop.

As you continue to show interest in their needs and eagerly provide helpful education (in various ways) concerning your products and services, they will increasingly **trust** you.

Trust is the most powerful force in the business universe. Trust secures the emotions of the buyer so that they become confident they are making the right decision to purchase your product or service.

If you don't touch their emotions, they're not going to open their wallets

Marketing guru Joe Sugarman astutely observed:

"People buy on emotion but they justify the purchase with logic."

The customer becomes emotionally connected to the "benefit" the product or service will give to them: prestige, convenience, recognition, free time, safety, etc. They then can find a dozen reasons why the product/service was such a logical choice.

We all do this, usually unconsciously, with almost everything we purchase.

That's why it is important for a business to "stack the benefits" of their product. Doing so brings down the purchase resistance of the customer because the customer can *logically* see that the *value* of the product far outweighs the purchase price.

Your customer is not buying your "stuff." Your customer is buying the *benefits* your "stuff" will provide for them.

Put another way, taking time to understand your prospect's real need is the key to him/her feeling understood and LIKING you for it.

Yet most businesses are so enamored with the "features" of their product or service that they are virtually out of touch with the real desire (benefit) in the customer's mind.

This is the reason that 61% of "satisfied customers" also said that they were 90% likely to purchase the same product/service *elsewhere* the next time! They had a "satisfactory" buying experience, but they were not "thrilled" with the experience.

"Satisfied customers" are NOT who you want buying your products and services. They are not loyal and have no conviction to continue with your company. But, "satisfied customers" is what the vast majority of businesses see as success. Let's hope they keep it up!

This "business-as-usual" approach now allows your company to exploit your competition's complacency and create an unfair advantage and an incredible opportunity by turning their "satisfied customers" into *thrilled* advocates, *devoted* clients and *raving* fans for YOUR company.

And the "Client Transfer Sequence" is just one of the many strategies we deploy in the...

Velocity Marketing System

Know, Like, Trust marketing (the Velocity System) is different and more effective than any "image" marketing system will ever be.

The Velocity System will deliver ideal prospects, predictably and dependably to your business. After being implemented, it will allow your business to run on autopilot and won't require a ton of labor on your part except for planned implementation of the strategies.

Know, Like, Trust marketing changes the *positioning* a business has in the marketplace. You must change the positioning so you're not chasing after clients; instead, you can actually structure the marketing strategies so the clients are coming to you.

Once clients start coming to you, because they know you "get" them, it's a completely different positioning. That's where all your leverage is.

That's why Velocity marketing utilizes a diversified group of systems that automatically delivers ideal prospects to your business (not tire kickers).

By "ideal prospects" I'm talking about prospects for your business that are pre-motivated, pre-qualified and pre-disposed to doing business with you.

That is so important because you won't be wasting time with people who don't want to spend their money with your business.

Additionally, once you have a streamlined marketing system in place, your advertising dollars will be super-charged instead of being wasted by "hope-this-works" advertising ideas that can't be effectively tracked or measured.

Instead, those valuable dollars and ads will be, implemented properly:

- they'll be cost justified;

- they'll be trackable;

- they'll be measurable, and

- they WILL drive ideal prospects to call you.

You won't have to go out beating the bushes trying to find prospects.

Each stage of the **Know, Like, Trust** chain reaction is triggered by sequentially implementing the marketing tools and systems that are designed for each stage of the process, building upon one another.

(Some of the key aspects of the sequence are covered in more detail in the chapters that follow in this book.)

Providing the proven tools and systems is where the Velocity Marketing System excels—benefits-focused marketing that "lights the fuse," igniting the **Know, Like, Trust** sequence that results in the potent chain reaction of astonishingly profitable after-effects.

2

How Do Your Customers See You?

Establishing a Positive Identity in the Minds of Your Customers

"Laughter is the shortest distance between two people."

– Victor Borge

Think of the word, "Professional." What image comes to your mind? Do you visualize a doctor, a dentist, a lawyer, or perhaps the president of a large corporation?

Did the image of the owner or manager of the business you operate cross your mind?

What criteria do you use to define a "professional?"

What about other people—your customers, for example?

How do you think they define a "professional?"

The services you perform for your customers on a daily basis can have a big impact on them, their family, their staff, employees or customers if they have businesses, and their financial futures.

The way you run your business and handle your customers' needs on a daily basis says a lot about you and the position you occupy in their minds.

In truth, your occupation should be viewed as being just as "professional" as that of any other, including doctors, dentists, lawyers, or any other type of business head.

The critical question is, how professionally do you perform within the scope of your occupation?

While this program is not a sales training course, it's important to know that no matter what your role in business is, you're involved in sales in one form or another.

And if you have staff or employees who are involved in sales, it's important for you to know the following information.

Five Types of Salespeople

Just as different salespeople have their own different and unique personalities, they also have different skill levels when it comes to selling and servicing their customers.

As we discuss the various types of salespeople and classify them according to their skill level, you will no doubt recognize some of the people you know or have encountered in the past. And as we do, take an honest look at yourself, to see where you might fit.

1. Professional Visitor

This person doesn't have any problem making appointments. In fact, they thrive on it. They enjoy visiting and talking to people, getting to know them, and may even engage in a casual discussion of their customers' problems.

Their conversation with a customer or prospect may or may not eventually involve the subject of how their products or services can benefit the buyers, and if it does, it usually has to be instigated by the customer or prospect.

A typical sales presentation will be oral, with very little (if any) use of visual materials, product brochures, or printed proposals.

2. Order Taker

These people don't mind talking to customers, clients or prospects, if they don't have to initiate the call. They are uncomfortable making appointments, and would rather have the customer or prospect come to them.

The telephone presents just as much a problem for these people. If the phone rings, they'll take the call and even discuss the customer's needs. But it's tough for them to pick up the receiver and dial a customer's number.

They operate best from a base of "low-price," and have difficulty handling objections. They would rather wait until someone asks for something specific, then they have no trouble filling the order.

3. Peddler

These are "sales-oriented" people. They have good product knowledge, but severely lack in "people skills." They operate from a sort of "hit-and-run" approach.

This person will assume a certain level of product knowledge on the part of the customer, and spend very little, if any, time establishing rapport with them. These people are either "product-oriented," or "price-oriented." Their entire presentation is based on product features or price, with little regard to how the product or service will benefit the customer.

The Peddler is the most prevalent type of salesperson you will find. Telemarketers who work the consumer market fit nicely into this category. It seems like it never fails. You may have just gotten home from a tough day at work and are relaxing with the kids, working in the yard, or perhaps even eating dinner.

Then the phone rings. It's for you. The person on the other end dives right into their presentation with no regard for the person they're calling.

For most people, especially professional salespeople, this inconvenience and the salesperson's level of incompetence is most aggravating. In these types of calls, the salesperson shows no concern for the prospect's time, inconvenience, present level of product knowledge, or whether or not there's any level of need, want or desire to know more about what they're selling.

The assumption is made by the caller that what he or she is offering the prospect in terms of a product, service or convenience is the same or better than what the prospect currently has, and that all the prospect is interested in is price. This type of approach is an insult to the prospect or customer, and is one of the biggest mistakes a salesperson can make.

4. Problem-Solver

These are salespeople who enjoy getting in front of people, ferreting out problems, needs and wants, and discussing workable solutions. They have empathy for the customer, can see the customer's needs *from the customer's point of view,* and enjoy helping the customer solve their problems.

The problem-solving person is good at establishing rapport with the prospect or customer, identifying what their needs, wants and desires are, developing creative, needs and wants-satisfying proposals, and making effective presentations.

But when it comes time to ask for the order, or close the sale, they tense up, lose their confidence, or otherwise fail to close the sale. Their customers or prospects, now having their needs identified and solutions presented, go elsewhere looking for a "better buy."

This salesperson has done all the work, and an Order-Taker for another company gets the sale—and the commission. After the Peddler, this is the next most common type of salesperson.

5. Counselor

In the business world, it's not uncommon for companies and corporations to have a staff of lawyers, or "legal counsel," on retainer to give advice in matters pertaining to the law, taxes, investments, mergers, or other difficult or legal situations.

The Counselor knows that when it comes to important buying decisions, his or her customers, be they companies, corporations, or individuals, should be no different.

To them, buying any type of product or service is a serious matter, not to be taken lightly, and can be an important tool for solving a need, satisfying a problem or adding to their profits, convenience or lifestyle.

They know that their customers need professional and qualified representation and advice, and the Counselor will do whatever it takes to provide it for them.

Like corporate legal counsel, this salesperson postures him or herself as being "on retainer," always available to give advice on matters pertaining to the products or services they sell. They make it clear in the customer's mind that there is absolutely no need for them to go anywhere else for answers to the problems their products or services can solve.

The Counselor knows how to establish rapport, build professional trust and credibility, identify their customer's current problems, develop effective proposals, offer credible and workable solutions, and make the presentation in such a way that their customers have no question in their minds but that they must buy the concepts they present, and hence, the product or service.

In addition, they have the ability to point out other, potential problems that the customer might encounter, and help them solve those needs as well.

This person operates much like a professional billiards champion. Before each shot, the billiards champion will carefully analyze the layout of the balls on the table, to see where the next two or three shots can best be made.

Then, with precision, he makes the shot at hand, and skillfully directs the cue ball to a predetermined spot so it is poised for the next shot.

Salespeople who function at this skill level also carefully review the customer's needs, both stated and unstated, and skillfully sets in motion, a plan to address those needs either now, or at a later, more convenient date.

Objections rarely come up because the Counselor has taken the time to anticipate what objections may arise, and then build the answers to the potential objections into his or her presentation.

This salesperson will get every drop of business the customer has, not because of price, but because the customer knows the salesperson really cares about them, understands their needs, and is willing to take the time to identify those needs and offer workable and credible solutions.

How Do Your Customers See You?

How do your customers see you? I mean, when the people you deal with on a regular basis, your customers and prospects—when they view you as the person they do, or are considering doing business with, who do they see?

Are you someone they might classify as a "typical salesperson"—someone who is out to sell them another product or service, or who is interested more in the sale or commission they'll earn?

Or, do your customers and prospects view you more as a counselor – someone they like and can relate to and who is genuinely interested in them, and making sure they have the right product for their individual and specific needs, at the best possible price? And in the event that what they've purchased does not, or will not work for them, or if you're not satisfied for any reason, will be behind you making things right?

How you answer this basic and important question is critical to your success in business. It can mean the difference between enormous success, mediocrity, or even dismal failure.

And, it's a self-feeding mechanism, as well. If you are viewed by your customers as a time waster or a product-hustler, even if it is not stated, you will tend to pick up that message yourself, and act accordingly, thus reinforcing your customer's image of you.

On the other hand, if your customers welcome you as a counselor, or an advisor—someone with their best interests in mind—someone who can help them identify and solve their problems, they will feel good about you. And consequently, you will also feel good about yourself, and the role you play relative to your customer. You will be and act more professional, more confident, and will be better able to help your customer with the solving of his or her needs and problems.

As you fill the role as a problem solver, you can't help but reinforce and strengthen that positive image in both you, and your customer's minds.

What Your Customers Really Want

As a businessperson, it is important for you to understand that only 35% of the reason people buy the products or services you offer, is for the actual product or service itself.

The other 65% of the reason they buy, is for what you can do or provide for your customer beyond the product or service, and what that product or service does for the customer.

In other words, if you are trying to sell your customers and prospects *products and services*, you are wasting your time. They are only 35% interested in *products and services.*

But they are 65% interested in the benefits of *having you involved.*

You see, chances are good that your customers and prospects can buy the same product or service (or at least comparable ones) from any one of several of your competitors.

And with that product or service, your competitor may offer a number of additional advantages, as well.

They may have a lower price, better quality product, some added bonuses or extra services, a location that's more convenient, or a payment plan that fits their budget better.

In today's tough, competitive market, it's difficult to compete on price or product. You may be able to command a certain advantage for a period time because you have a lower price than your competitors, but you and I both know that it will be short-lived.

The truth is, you will never be able to maintain a competitive position in the marketplace – long-term for any length of time because of the prices you charge or the products you provide.

It'll just be a matter of time before either one of your competitors lowers their prices or duplicates (or even betters) your product, or you raise your prices because you no longer have the necessary margins to justify your prices.

But there's one thing your customers can't get from any of your competitors. And that's you, and the empathy, the problem solving expertise and the knowledge, education and commitment to service that you bring to his or her specific and unique situation.

Products and Services—or Advice?

So it is important to continually ask yourself (and be honest) the following question…

"How do your customers…the people who do business with you…your clients and prospects, see you?"

On the next page is an example of an easy method you can use to find out.

Take a sheet of paper and draw a line down the middle.

On the left hand side at the top, label the column, "Products and Services."

Label the right hand column, "Help and Advice."

Every time you are in contact with a customer or prospect, whether they call you or you have a face-to-face meeting, evaluate the overall purpose of the meeting.

Products and Services	Help and Advice

Did your customer or prospect look to you for the products or services you provide? Or did they seek your help, advice or counsel to help them make a decision that would solve a particular need or challenge they were encountering?

Once you've determined that, place a mark in the appropriate column. Then at the end of the month, evaluate the results of your list.

If you have more marks in the "Products and Services" column than in the "Help and Advice" column, you pretty well know what perception your customers have of you.

But equally important, you also know what you need to do to change that perception. You can then begin to develop and implement a plan of action that focuses on improving your image in the eyes of your customers. Then test yourself again several months later. By comparing your evaluation sheets over the period of a year or two, you can easily see the progress you're making.

Improvement is not always difficult. Oftentimes, a person may not know where they are weak or where they need to improve. But if you can isolate those areas that need improvement, you can then begin to take the necessary steps to effect positive change.

3

How Much Are You Worth?

Strategies for Determining and Increasing Your Value to Your Customers

---

"Live out of your imagination, not your history."

– Stephen Covey

You are in business for yourself. That is, you may own your own business, or you may be associated with another company or firm, either as an employee, a partner or an independent contractor. Your working agreement or arrangement doesn't really matter.

The important thing to realize is that no matter what the arrangement or situation you presently find yourself in, you are really working for yourself. If you work by commission, for example, the sales you make are not only putting dollars in your employer's pocket, they are putting dollars into your own pocket, as well. The more you sell, the more you make.

Just consider yourself as a business that prospers or falters financially by the amount of commission dollars you generate. The point is, even though you may be working for, or associated with another company or concern, you are really working for yourself to increase the amount of money you earn for you.

Three Keys for Success

It's important to realize that your success in whatever you do in business, or in life, for that matter, will always be determined by three things:

1. **The need or demand for what you do,**

2. **Your ability to do it, and**

3. **The difficulty in replacing you.**

In other words, how valuable are you and the service you perform, to other people?

To illustrate this point, let's apply our 3-step formula to the job of an elevator operator. In today's world of pushbutton, self-operated elevators, how much need is there for the job he or she performs?

Most people are quite capable of operating an elevator themselves. It doesn't take much knowledge or training, so an operator can be replaced without much difficulty. As a result, elevator operators, if you can even find one, are not paid much.

Now, contrast the elevator operator and the money he or she commands with that of a professional major league baseball player. Specifically, a player that is good at batting.

What is the *need for what they do?* A look at attendance figures for baseball games will show that more than just a few fans are interested in watching what they do. So the need obviously is great.

How about the batter's *ability to do what he does?* Sports analysts say that the action of hitting a ball moving towards you at over 90 miles per hour is the single most difficult movement in sports.

In the game of basketball, the target (the hoop) doesn't move. Same in golf. While the ball moves, the hole, or goal, remains stationary. In football, there are 11 teammates all with a common goal of advancing the ball. But in baseball, it's the batter alone, trying to hit a small, 90 M.P.H. target with his bat. So it stands to reason then, that the better or more often a batter can hit the ball, the more he or she will be compensated.

Now, what about the *difficulty in replacing* a good batter? When only the best in the world can hit the target less than a third of the time, and most of the other players are successful far less than that, it doesn't take long to realize why the best batters are among the highest moneymakers in the world.

Obtaining Superior Rewards

Now how about you? It's been said, that you can tell how professional a person is by the size of their income at the end of the year.

And you can tell exactly how valuable the service you perform is, by how much people are willing to pay you for it. If you do the same job that everybody else does, and do it no better than the way they do it, you can't expect to earn more money, or be considered any more valuable than those other people. You see, the market, by nature, will pay superior rewards only for superior goods and services. It will pay average rewards for average goods and services, and it will see that inferior rewards are paid for inferior goods and services.

In other words, you will be rewarded in direct proportion to the value you provide your customers. It's inescapable. That's the law of nature.

Now, if the products and services you sell or provide are similar in coverage and price to everyone else's (and most of them are, today), then the difference between you and other people in your position has to be in the type and amount of personal service you provide your customers and clients.

This, then, has to be the area you excel in—it becomes your competitive edge.

Guaranteeing Business Success

So one of the main keys to success in business, then, is, number one, to make sure that there is a great *need or demand for what you do.*

One of the best ways to guarantee that is to make sure you only spend your time selling to qualified prospects. That is, people who need, want and can pay for what you're selling. There may be people who need or want what you have, but if they can't afford to pay for it, or if you can't arrange suitable payment options for them, you'll spend a seemingly endless amount of time and get nowhere.

On the other hand, there may be people who have the ability to pay, but not the need or want. In these cases, you can also waste considerable time, because surely, no sale will result from your efforts.

The second point is that you are paid in direct proportion to your *ability to do what it is that you do.* That is, to identify, qualify and sell the products and services you offer to your prospects and customers, and then service their needs as they arise.

In some businesses, the sole function of salespeople is to seek out qualified prospects and sell them the products or services offered by the business. The necessary service work for the customer is provided by an office or support staff.

In other businesses, each salesperson is responsible in every way for each of their customer's needs, from the initial sale, to providing all the necessary service the customer might require, including updating the product or service, customer complaints, changes of address, or any other service work that may be needed.

The determining factor then, is not what your responsibilities are, but rather, how good you are at performing those responsibilities.

Third, remember, that you are paid in direct proportion to the difficulty *in replacing you.*

When I think of this area, I think of Disneyland and Disneyworld. As attractions go, they have very little competition. And as far as theme parks? They are unsurpassed. Their average daily attendance figures bear this out.

Disneyland — California: 44,000

Disneyworld, Epcot Center — Florida: 82,329

Disneyland — Tokyo: 40,677

With 167,000 guests visiting each day, and paying an average of $100 per person, the Disney properties are light years ahead of their nearest competition. And, why? Because they have met the criteria outlined in the 3-step formula.

Let's consider each of the steps of the formula as they apply to Disney.

First, is there a need for what they do? Certainly there must be. Entertainment is the largest and fastest growing business in the world today, both in terms of participants, and in total dollar revenue.

Next, how about Disney's ability to do what they do? With over 53 million people visiting their 3 parks each year, evidence would indicate that they are doing at least a few things, if not a whole lot of things right.

And finally, the difficulty in replacing them? Nothing has come close yet, and with those 53 million people spending over $6 billion, odds are that the people who visit the Disney properties are pretty satisfied.

The Law of Unlimited Abundance

Walt Disney was a man of extraordinary vision and foresight. He knew what it would take to be successful in his chosen area of business, and he developed a formula that expressed his philosophy, and could be used in any type of business to ensure its success. He called it, his "Law of Unlimited Abundance."

Walt said that it didn't matter what type of business or endeavor a person was engaged in, they could be successful and enjoy *unlimited abundance*, if they would simply follow his formula or plan.

Walt Disney's "Law of Unlimited Abundance," stated, that to be successful, you must,

"Do what you do so well, that the people who see you do it, will want to see you do it again, and will bring others to see you do it."

That's the credo that built the enormous successes of Disneyland and Disneyworld. And in their arena of operation, they stand alone.

Disney's Law Can Work for You!

It can be similar in your business world, too. You see, the key is to, "*do what you do,*" not what someone else does, but what *you* do. You don't have to copy. You simply do your job the way only you can. That's what makes you special, sets you apart from others, and attracts people to you.

Then you do what you do, "*so well,*" that is, provide the type of service your customers require, want, or need in an exceptional manner. It leaves no room for mediocrity, it's "so well." That implies exceptional performance.

And if you will do that so, "*the people who see you do it,*" (your customers), "*will want to see you do it again,*" (that's repeat business), "*and will bring others to see you do it,*" (that's referral business), you too, can meet with an unparalleled success.

Because so few people perform in business that way, it sets you completely apart from all the competition. Customers can't get the kind of service you offer from anyone or anywhere else. It's simply not available anywhere, at any price.

So, by default, you become unique, different, and difficult to replace. And it will be reflected in your business and your income. It has to. There's no choice. It is a basic, eternal law of nature. You simply reap the results of what you've sown.

You Reap What You Sow

The question you must answer in your mind Is, "What are you going to sow, so you will reap the kinds of rewards you wish to have?"

In the world of business, this is a most critical question, and one you would do well to take the time to answer. Fact is, most business people simply don't understand how important the answer to this one question really is.

You see, many people go into business because it is something they have always wanted to do, or because they want a certain amount of freedom. Perhaps they want to be their own boss.

Now, those are not necessarily bad reasons, but they are selfish reasons for the most part, and while they may sound good on the surface, in actuality, some of them may not be very practical.

If you go into business for selfish reasons, and fail to give the customer his or her rightful due, your chances of success are likely to meet with hard times.

Business, like farming, requires that you do certain things in a particular order, if you are to realize an abundant harvest. Now the answer to the question,

"What are you going to sow, so you will reap the kinds of rewards you want?"

...is simple. You only have to look at the question backwards.

First, what kinds of rewards do you want? Second, what do you have to do to get those rewards? And third, who is it that can give you those rewards?

If you will always remember, that although you may own, or work for, or represent a certain company, they are not who pays you.

The Customer Signs Your Paycheck

It really is the customer that signs your paycheck. And although you must see that your company's interests are always considered, you must not lose sight that the customer is the boss.

They are the whole reason your job exists in the first place. They hire you to help them make good personal and business decisions. They trust you to help them see that their problems or needs are solved or satisfied in an efficient and cost-effective manner, and they pay you well to do your job. It is the wants, needs and desires of your customers that should determine all of your business activity. So the next logical step then, is to learn and understand just what your customer's wants, needs and desires are. And you find that out simply by interviewing and asking them. It is very important to listen carefully to what they say because sometimes there may be other, hidden or unstated wants or needs that may not be readily evident. And only by fully understanding their needs, can you be of meaningful service to them.

4

Why People Buy

*Identifying the Basic Motives That Make
Your Customers Want To Buy*

**"Life is a series of problems. Do we want to
moan about them or solve them?"**

– M. Scott Peck

People don't buy for the sake of owning a certain product or service. Rather, they buy because of the benefits they will receive as a result of owning that product or service.

The example that has traditionally been used to illustrate this point, is that one year, a quarter of a million quarter-inch drills were sold, and not one person that bought a drill wanted a quarter-inch drill. Instead, they bought the drills because they wanted the benefits the drill could provide... a hole.

People buy your products and services for the same reason... not for a hole... but for the benefits those products or services provides. Ask the next 10 prospects you come in contact with if they want to buy the product or service you're selling, and chances are, you'll receive a negative answer.

There are many factors that influence people to react that way, and each person has his or her own reasons for doing so. Regardless of individual reasons, it's a fact that people don't want to buy *products*, and they often resent people trying to sell them

People Buy for the Benefits

On the other hand, if you ask the same person that previously turned you down if they want the specific benefits the products or services you're selling will provide them, you will most likely receive a positive answer. They may give you a hard time about the prices you are charging, but in most cases, the answer will be a "yes."

Like the quarter-inch drills, people are not interested in products, but they are interested in the benefits the products will provide them. It makes sense then, that when you are making a presentation, that you don't emphasize *products.*

Rather, you should talk in terms of *specific benefits,* and how those benefits apply directly to the particular prospect in front of you at the time.

> As mentioned previously, each person is different, and each person has his or her own reasons for buying or not buying. And each person will buy for his or her own reasons – not yours or anyone else's.

If you try to sell them for any reason other than their own, you run the risk of turning them off or otherwise alienating them, which usually ends up destroying the sale you are trying to make, as well as any future sales.

Trying to figure out why people make certain decisions can be a complicated, even frustrating process, at best. But an understanding of basic buying motives can make your job much easier.

Motives for Buying

Behavioral psychologists tell us there are seven basic motives that move a person to action – that cause them to buy. An understanding of these motives and how they apply to your customers and prospects at the time a buying decision is being made, can give you a tremendous advantage.

1. Desire for Gain or Profit
Nobody likes to lose. People want something in return for their efforts and hard work. And the

easier they can get it, the better. The success of the lottery games in various states bear testimony of people trying to find an easy way to get gain and profit.

The products you sell, can help your customers realize their dreams for gain or profit, too. Your customers can and will invest in various types of products or services you sell – not to own them, per se, but in an effort to increase their profitability and the amount and value of their assets.

2. Fear of Loss, or Need For Security

People will go to great lengths to prevent losing something. In an effort to protect their property, some people install burglar or fire alarms, smoke detectors, or nightlights that auto-matically come on when movement is detected.

Some people carry spray cans of mace, or tear gas, while others have resorted to carrying guns or other weapons to protect their person.

Psychologists say that the fear of loss or the need for security is perhaps, the greatest of all the motives.

If the products and services you sell can help protect your clients, their families or their businesses from loss, or if you can in some way increase their security, either at the present time or sometime in the future, you owe it to them to capitalize on that fact as much and as often as possible.

3. Pride of Ownership, Or Status

People want to be noticed and recognized. Little boys ride bicycles with no hands, and little girls dress up and act out dance routines and shout to their parents, "Watch me! Watch me!"

Adults do the same things, but in different ways. While they may not verbally shout out, they still say "Watch me! Watch me!" just as loudly.

They do it by the kinds of cars they drive, the clothes and jewelry they wear, the houses they live in, and the material things they possess.

While people may buy because of the benefits, they like others to see the actual product. In some cases, it's just another way to say, "Watch me! Watch me!"

4. An Interest in Doing Something Easier or More Efficiently

We all want methods of doing things easier. One only has to look around his or her home to notice the abundance of time and/or money-saving conveniences we all enjoy.

What about your products or services?

Do they somehow make a person's job, or a business' way of doing things easier or more efficient?

And if they do, what are the direct and indirect benefits to your prospect or customer?

Is this something you can capitalize on?

5. The Desire for Excitement or Pleasure

The message is clear that people want excitement and pleasure. And it seems to suggest that pleasure comes in the "having," rather than in the "getting."

But in reality, "excitement" and "pleasure," for most people comes in the acquiring of things.

Think back about the times you have worked hard to get something, and how excited you were in the process.

But then, once you had whatever it was that you were working for, how the excitement was dulled.

Sometimes it's not the end result that counts as much as the process of acquiring.

Of course, these applications have to do with "things." Some people really enjoy acquiring "things," and even keep score by how much they accumulate.

Other people gain great pleasure or excitement knowing that their family's future educational and livings needs, as well as retirement will be taken care of.

Business owners like to know that their businesses are operating at peak efficiency and profitability, and are meeting the needs of their customers, and as a result, will be around for long time providing jobs and security for their employees and their families, as well as providing retirement funds for the owner when the business is sold.

6. Self-Improvement or an Increase in Effectiveness

Your investment of both money and time in this book is a good example of your desire for self-improvement and increased effectiveness. People want and need to improve and to be able to do things more efficiently.

Sometimes that involves taking risks with time or money. Not all risks have to be "risky." Calculated risks based on well thought-out plans and outcomes are the safest way to go, and can contribute greatly to the successful improvement in effectiveness and efficiency.

7. The Desire for Importance or the Need to Feel Appreciated

According to noted psychiatrist, Dr. Abraham Maslow, this is one of the basic needs of all humans; acceptance and appreciation. Children want to be accepted by their parents and peers, and parents want their children to remember them when they grow up and leave home.

In his book, *The Human Side of Enterprise,* Douglas McGregor explains that workers are motivated more by "significant works," and a feeling of being needed and appreciated, than by money.

People want to make a difference, and be appreciated for it. Fathers and mothers not only have an obligation to see that their family's futures are provided for, but they want their family to understand and appreciate their efforts.

Business owners have an obligation to the people who buy from them, the employees who work for them, their employees' families, the suppliers and the vendors who sell to them. Too often, each of those groups of people live with an attitude of expectancy and entitlement. That is, they expect that the business owner will take care of them. How much better it would be if more appreciation would be shown to those who make our lives better.

If the products or services you provide the marketplace can help make this possible, you may have an open ticket to success because of the great unsatisfied need that exists.

If you understand these basic motives and how they apply to your business of selling your products and services, and then sell to the needs (both stated and unstated) of your customers and prospects, you will prosper.

And if you are not prospering, it simply means you have not uncovered your prospect's and customer's motives for buying. You are not addressing their specific needs. In most cases, you can't wait for your customers to tell you what they want. You have to be able to recognize their needs.

Remember, you are ultimately responsible for the success or failure of your business. If you are doing it right or wrong, either way, the marketplace will let you know.

The Loyalty of the Customer

Customers make an interesting study. It seems that they always want the very most for the very least they'll have to pay. They are ruthless, selfish, demanding and disloyal.

You know the story. You've done business with someone for several years and they've been good customers. You've given them the best service possible and you think they are your customers for life. But then some little thing possibly out of your control goes wrong, or they see an ad or get a call from a competitor, someone they've never met before, with a slightly lower price, and the next thing you know, they are gone, oftentimes without a single word to you.

At first you don't notice it. But one day you realize that it's been a while since you've seen or heard from that customer. When you find out what happened, you feel badly, because if they would have just called you, you might have been able to make a couple of changes and save the business. But it's too late, they're gone.

This scenario is repeated time and again with businesses owners from every company, who sell every type of product or service. It is going to happen. To pretend that it doesn't, or won't happen, is simply deceiving yourself.

It's incredible how many business owners just write off the loss of a good customer. But that's not the thing you should do. Instead, now is the time to become even more proactive and go after that "lost" customer.

One of the best ways to minimize or cut down on the frequency of losing your good customers, is to resell them on the reasons they bought from you in the first place. Regularly scheduled meetings or conversations with your customers to remind them of their motives can go a long way in helping insulate your business from the competition.

Remember, that your competition has similar products, services and prices. Also remember that your customer's reasons for buying are only 35 percent based on those products, services, and prices. The other 65 percent is for what you can do for them.

Spend the time with them. Review their needs, wants and concerns. Remind them why they bought from you in the first place. Reinforce their motives, and their decisions for buying, and you will reduce your customer defection rate and develop not only loyal customers, but friends, as well.

5

The Main Purpose
of Your Business

*Getting and Keeping
Customers…Profitability Is Priority
Number One*

**"In every difficult situation is potential value.
Believe this, then begin looking for it."**

– Norman Vincent Peale

When you have an effective system that will allow you to *profitably* get and keep *quality* customers that will return to do business with you over and over again, and then actively and enthusiastically refer you to others, your business will produce more profits than you can possibly imagine. And then everything else falls into place.

On the other hand, if you don't have enough customers buying from you or using your services regularly, then you'll not likely stay in business for very long, and will never have the chance to make a profit.

Now, let's take a minute and look closely at the individual components of this important business skill...

Knowing How to Profitably Attract Quality Customers

Customers are the lifeblood of any business. Without customers buying the products and services you have to offer, you wouldn't have a business to begin with. But customers alone, aren't enough.

You want *quality* customers... customers who are pleasant to deal with. Customers who return to repurchase from you again and again. Customers who you can sell to and realize a reasonable profit from.

And you want to be able to *profitably* attract them. In other words, the return you realize from your investment of advertising or marketing dollars to acquire new customers, should be positive. You want a positive R.O.I., or return on your investment.

Next, you want to...

Ethically Exploit Their Maximum Financial Potential

Each of your customers has certain needs and wants. And the more of those needs and wants you can handle for them, the more benefits you can provide them, and the more profits you'll realize.

It should be your goal to sell as many products and services to your customers as they need.

You shouldn't take advantage of them or your relationship with them, but you should make every effort to sell them everything that you can *ethically* justify selling them.

It really comes down to this, and I'll speak very frankly. If you really do provide the best products and services in the marketplace (if you don't, you'd better rethink your ethics and why you're in business), and if you really are the business who can serve your customers' needs better than anyone else (and if you're not, you either need to become that business or get out of the business), then you have a moral and an ethical responsibility to make sure that every one of your customers at least has the opportunity to take advantage of them.

And you should do everything in your power that's *reasonable* and *ethical* to give them that opportunity.

Next you want to…

Convert Your Customers to Advocates Who Actively and Enthusiastically Refer You to Others

By definition, an "advocate" is someone who is a backer, a supporter, a promoter, a believer, an activist, a campaigner, a sponsor.

The last thing you need is a database full of one-product, or one-service customers who buy the minimum amount from you, complain about your prices every time they make a purchase, and give the rest of their business to the company or business who has the lowest prices or a "better deal."

There's no way you can make a profit on these types of customers. Besides, they make your life miserable and drive you crazy in the process.

Who you want are customers who not only give you all (or the majority) of their business, but re-buy from you repeatedly, year after year. You want customers that are so happy and so pleased with what you do for them that they actively and enthusiastically campaign for you. That the story they tell about you, is so compelling that the people they tell are nearly forced to call you and ask for your help. Those are the people who make your job fun, enjoyable and profitable.

And finally, you want to…

Keep Your Customers for Life

Reliable studies demonstrate that the more needs a business handles for a customer, the longer they can expect that customer to do business with them.

In the insurance business for instance, an agent increases his chances of keeping an insured for three years or more by the following percentages:

- 45% if the agent insures only the auto policies

- 50% if both the auto and home owners policies are insured

- 60% with auto, homeowners and life policies, and

- **97% with auto, homeowners, life and health policies!**

While these figures are illustrative of the insurance business, the same principle is true of most other businesses. Banks, for instance, have studies that show the difference in customer retention with a customer that only has a checking account, versus another customer with multiple checking accounts, a savings account, an IRA, Safety Deposit box, their car financed through the bank, and a number of other services.

The idea is that by serving all the needs your prospects or customers have, with the products and services you provide or have access to, you lock yourself in and the competition out.

And obviously, the longer you retain your customers, the more income you will earn from them, the more chances you will have to sell them additional products and services, and the more referrals you can get from them. It all adds up to increased profits for you.

Retention of your customers... the ones you've spent so much time, effort and money attracting and convincing to do business with you is critically important.

More than one study suggests that it costs six times more to get a prospect to buy from you than it does to get an existing customer to purchase from you again, and that it's sixteen times easier to sell an existing customer than it is a new prospect.

When you add it all up, for every 5% increase in customer retention, you'll generate a 30% to 45% increase in profitability over an 18-month period.

Depending on the nature of the products and services you sell, if your repurchase rate isn't in the high 90 percentile range, you have some work to do.

A lost customer is more than just a lost customer, and their attending profits. It's much more. In future chapters, we'll be discussing how to determine what the actual cost of a lost customer is, and what to do to prevent them from leaving.

But for now, just keep this important point in mind... if you're going to be successful in business, no matter what type of products or services you sell, you've got to have an intense focus on your customer. You've got to find out what they want and do everything you can to help them get it.

And if you want to make a fortune rather than just a living, you can't do it for only a few. You must do it for large numbers of people.

The success of your business will depend on how well you serve your customers... the people who buy from you!

6

The Four Primary Ways
To Grow Your Business

*Maximizing the Return on Your
Efforts in the Four Key and
Critical Areas*

**"Our deeds determine us as much as we
determine our deeds."**

– George Eliot

The number one thing... and one of the most important things for any business owner, manager, entrepreneur or professional to realize, is that there are four ways... four *principal* ways to grow a business – any business.

There are many things you can do to grow your business, but for purposes of our discussion here, we'll be focusing on four primary things.

The truth is, that other than some administrative functions, some of which are not under your direct influence or control, nearly everything you do to build or grow your business can be classified under one of four different and distinct areas, or categories, and if you learn this one simple concept and how to apply it, believe me, your competition won't stand a chance.

And the reason?

Because your competition not only doesn't understand this concept, most of them have never even heard of it.

Now, here's the first one of the four ways to grow your business. Simply…

Get More Customers

That's it. Build your customer base. Get more prospects to buy from you and become your customers.

You know how it works. When more people buy from you, you take in more gross dollars, and as a result (depending on your margins and overhead), you make more bottom line profits.

As a spin-off benefit, the more people you add to your customer base the larger it becomes, and the larger it becomes the more people you have to go back to for additional sales and the referrals they're capable of giving you.

It's in this one single area where most business owners (including your competition, and probably, you, too, if you're honest), spend most of their time, effort and money.

If you've been in business for any length of time, you probably realize that getting new customers is not always the easiest, the most time-efficient, or most profitable thing you can do.

Most businesses only have one or two main methods of attracting new prospects to their businesses.

For example, you probably know that a large number of businesses are heavy in the use of telephone soliciting.

In fact, you, yourself, have probably gotten more than your fair share of calls, when you were just sitting down for dinner.

Chiropractors, car dealers, truck driving schools, and lawyers take a different approach. Many of them advertise heavily on television, especially during the afternoon hours to attract new customers. They've found that a large part of their intended audience... the people who are most inclined to use their services, watch television during those hours, and it's a cost-effective way to reach them.

Each business, industry, or profession has their own methods and timing to contact those who are most likely to be interested in their products and services. What works for some businesses, may or may not work for other businesses in the same or different industries or professions.

Think about your business and your company for a minute. Chances are, that you, like nearly every other business owner in your industry or profession also utilizes one, or perhaps two main methods of attracting new prospects.

Most likely, the method you use is the same method that nearly every other business uses. It's called the, *"That's how things are done in our industry or profession,"* method.

Typically, when a person first chooses to go into business they look around and see what everyone else is doing.

Then they layout their office, shop or place of business just like every other similar type of business they've seen.

They look at what everyone else is doing to market or promote their businesses, products and services, and adopt those same marketing plans and methods to market or promote their business.

This activity isn't isolated to just a few businesses – nearly every business in nearly every industry or profession is guilty.

But, wait a minute. Who set up that system in the first place? And who says it's right, or that it's the best system for you to use? The fact is, that there are an unlimited number of methods of attracting new customers to your business, and your imagination is the only limiting factor.

Some of the best, most productive and cost-effective methods you can use, can be adapted from what others are doing in totally unrelated businesses.

Now, this brings up a couple of questions. First, how observant are you? What are others who are in the same business that you're in doing? And, how effective are they?

Next, look around at what other businesses... unrelated businesses in other, unrelated fields, industries or professions are doing. Have you seen what's working for them? Is there one business that just stands out, by doing something different or unusual? Or, do they all pretty much use the same marketing methods?

Next question: How creative are you? Can you look at what some of the other businesses are doing, and adapt (with a few minor changes), their methods to your business?

In other words, if you were brand new, just starting in business, and had no idea of what anyone before you had done to attract new customers, what would you do? How would you go about getting new customers? Would you use the same methods you use now, or would you do something completely different?

I know of a dentist who specializes in working with children and their teeth. He loves children. And he recognizes that as they get older, they may need braces, they'll probably get married, and have a spouse and children that will all need dental care.

So, he set up his reception room with a special, "kid-height" counter, so when the children come in, they can talk directly to the receptionist, transact their business just as an adult would, and schedule their next appointment. He's even decorated his reception area with artwork and pictures that some of his young patients have created.

How do you think those young people feel? Well, you probably guessed it. They absolutely love it there. And they tell their friends about it, too. And their parents? They're *thrilled*.

Imagine, having your kids *want* to go to the dentist! And then be treated, not like a second-class citizen, but as an equal, transacting business (with the parent's help, of course), and having a hand in scheduling their future appointments.

What a learning and growing experience for them. And who do you think the parents use for their own dentist? That's right.

The spin-off business of catering to, and working with children, is their parents.

As the kids grow up and have families of their own, which dentist do you think they'll use... that they'll insist their spouse switches to, and that they'll bring their own children to?

The relationship this dentist is building with those young people... of friendship, of trust and of caring, will provide him all the financial security he'll ever need, and allow him to do whatever he wants, and go wherever he pleases for the rest of his life.

So, what about you and your business? What are you doing? Specifically, what marketing methods are you using, *right now* to attract new customers, and to build lasting relationships with them so they'll do business with you for a lifetime?

Second, how many *different* marketing methods do you presently, and concurrently, have working for you? There's a real danger in having just one or two main methods of attracting new customers.

One business depended almost entirely on a telemarketing team to acquire leads for their salespeople to follow up with. When a well-funded competitor opened for business not far away, they hired nearly all that business' telemarketing staff, and nearly shut the business down. The business was nearly a total disaster.

When they finally called in a consultant friend of mine, it was clear that the company needed to do something quick, just to save the business. They got to work and hired and trained a whole new telemarketing crew, and got the business up and running again.

But then they looked at other marketing options and put together an effective direct-mail program, started a proactive referral-generating system, and worked out some joint ventures and host-beneficiary relationships with other, complementary, but non-competing businesses.

Now, if something happens to any one of their marketing methods, they have other strategies or other "pillars" in place that can keep the business from collapsing, and keep it running smoothly.

What about your business? How can you apply this?

Well, why not start by going back and revisiting the questions I asked earlier. Then see if there are some areas that you need to improve in.

Make sure you're not dependent on only one or two main methods of attracting new customers.

New customers are important to your business, there's no question. But, they're not just important, they're absolutely vital... not only to the growth of your business, but to the very survival of the business.

It's critical that you have multiple systems in place to ensure that your business continues running, *and growing*, uninterrupted, if anything unexpected happens.

Because of the limited amount of space in these pages, we can't talk about all the methods of getting new customers, but in the training materials and workshops we conduct, we go into great detail on effective ways to attract prospects by the bushel, and convert them into loyal, long-term customers.

As important as getting more new customers is, there are still three more methods you can use to grow your business. And each of these methods are more profitable, more effective, and give you greater potential for leverage than the first method.

Let's talk about number two...

Get Your Customers to Make Larger Average Purchases

In other words, increase the average transactional value of their purchases. Or more simply, get them to spend more money when they buy something from you.

This just happens to be the quickest and easiest way there is to increase your profits. One of the things that continually amazes me, is the number of businesses that have *extensive* and *expensive* plans in place to acquire more customers.

Yet, very few have paid much attention to this highly profitable, and highly leveragable step of increasing the size of the order... getting more money from each of your customers every time they buy from you.

If you think for a minute, about how easy this is and how profitable it can be, you'll see why it's such a powerful concept. And, you'll also see why nearly every fast-food restaurant has embraced, has mastered, and requires that every person who takes orders, understands, and is proficient in the use of the "up-sell" and "cross-selling" principles.

Think back about your own fast-food restaurant experience. You drive up to the speaker and place your order... a sandwich and a drink. And then what happens? A voice comes back over the speaker and asks if you'd like an apple pie, or fries with your order.

That's an example of cross-selling. Selling an additional product in addition to, or beyond the initial purchase.

Or, they might suggest that you "super-size" or "giant-size" your order. That's an example of an up-sell... increasing the size of the initial order.

In any case, if you take them up on their suggestion, what they've done is just increase their profits *substantially*, since they made an additional sale, but had no acquisition or marketing costs.

You see, they realize, that a certain percentage of their customers will say, "Yes." And the only reason they say, "Yes," is because a suggestion was made to them. So they play the numbers game.

And the result? Well, by being aware of what their customers might want, but not ask for on their own, and then by asking questions or making suggestions, they bring in a substantial number of dollars. And other than the actual cost of the product, those dollars are pure profit.

Here's another technique fast food restaurants frequently use. It's called "bundling," or "packaging."

It's where they combine a sandwich, a drink and fries, then throw in a couple of "bonus" items, like maybe a cookie and a toy. They put it all together in one package, and give it a name like, "Happy Meal."

They'll charge you less for that package than what each of those items purchased separately would have cost, but the total dollar amount you spend will be higher.

And, since there were no marketing costs involved, other than the cost of the items, themselves, it's pure profit, and it goes straight to their bottom line.

Now, what does that have to do with you, and your business?

Well, you may not be in the fast food business, but the same principles can still apply. Just ask yourself this question: "What additional products or services do you have that would be natural complements to what your customers initially buy from you?"

Well, you know the answer to that and I won't go into all the details here. But for instance, if you have the type of business that offers more than one product to your customers you have a tremendous advantage to capitalize on the up-selling, cross-selling and bundling techniques.

Some types of businesses, such as insurance companies that may offer only one product or service can also benefit from these strategies by packaging certain policies that cover multiple family members, adding riders, or including other complementary services that go beyond the actual policies themselves.

Do these things seem like common sense to you? Well, they probably do. But as I mentioned before, it's surprising how few businesses make effective use these three simple principles.

Think about it. In reality, you have an obligation to your customers... the people who trust you to provide them good quality products and services, give them sound advice and who hand over their hard-earned money to you... to make sure they get the very best value, the best use and the most enjoyment from their original purchase.

And if you have additional items, either products or services, that can enhance their value, their use or their enjoyment, then your obligation is to do everything that's reasonable and ethical, to see that they at least have the option of taking advantage of those items.

Again, it's playing the numbers game. Some will take advantage of your offer, and some won't. But at least, you will have given them the opportunity, and you will have fulfilled your obligation to them.

You haven't made the decision for them. You've given them a choice, and you've let them decide.

If you come across as sincere, they'll not see you as being pushy, but they'll realize that you are really trying to do them a favor... to help them get more value, more use, and more benefit from their decision and their purchase.

And they'll come back to do business with you again, and again, and will refer others to you, as well.

Up-selling, cross-selling and bundling... these are only three of more than a dozen immediate, profit-producing methods you can use to skyrocket your business to the next level.

If you do nothing more than find a way to incorporate these three techniques in your business (which you should be able to do within the next twenty-four hours), you'll blast your profits completely through the roof.

Think about it... increasing your sales... increasing your *profits*... without increasing your expenses. It's an exciting concept, and it can add an *immediate* twenty, thirty, even forty percent or more, *in pure profits* to your bottom line!

Now, let's move on to the third way to grow your business...

Get Your Customers to Buy From You More Often

In other words, increase the frequency of their purchases. Get them to come back, Give them reasons to *want* to come back and to continue doing business with you. The longer your customers go between purchases from you, the more chance they have of buying from your competition.

It's like, "Out of sight, out of mind." You need to constantly stay in front of your customers with educational information, and notices of changes in the law or updates regarding the products or services they've purchased from you that can affect them. And you need to tell them about new products, new lines, special incentives and other offers that might benefit them.

The idea, is two-fold: One, to "lock" your customers in, so they can't afford to do business with anyone else, and secondly, to make it so attractive to do business with you, that they wouldn't even consider going anywhere else.

What you really want to do, is lead your customers to the inescapable and undeniable conclusion, that they would have to be completely out of their minds to even consider doing business with anyone else but you, regardless of the selection of products or services you provide, the prices you charge, your location, or the relationship they may have with the business they're currently doing business with.

Let me give you a real life example of how this can work for a restaurant owner. For his business customers who like to take their clients to lunch, he offers a certain number of lunches for a pre-paid, discounted price.

By doing this, he "locks in" his customer, gets his money up-front, and makes it convenient for everyone. The customer simply signs the check, which includes the tip. No money changes hands during or after the lunch, and new customers are constantly being introduced to his restaurant. As a result, many of those new customers take advantage of the same arrangement for their clients.

Here's another example. I've patronized car washes that offer a pre-paid, discounted card, that's good for a certain number of car washes. It's a great deal because the customers save money and can take their car to be washed even if they don't have any money with them.

And, when the card is filled, customers have a free wax job coming. It's a good deal for the car wash too, because they've gotten their money up front and have locked their customers out of the competition.

Airlines offer upgrades and mileage bonuses for those who fly with them on a regular basis. And countless other businesses offer similar programs, as well.

Now, let's apply this concept to you and your business. What can you think of that you could do, that will endear your customers to you? To lock them in, and get them coming back more often, and even refer others to do business with you?

Do you have an educational newsletter or special informative reports that you periodically send them that keeps them updated?

Do you send postcards, or do you have a website that keeps them informed of new items and promotions?

Do you hold special "Customer Appreciation Sales" or events?

How about a frequent buyer club for your more loyal customers?

What about a Referral Reward system that recognizes or compensates your customers for referring their friends?

You've got to let your customers know that you value them, that you appreciate them, that you want them to come back, and you want to make doing business with you fun, risk-free, rewarding, and easy.

Well, I'm sure you can see that the ideas are unlimited. And while the restaurant, car wash and shoe store examples may not apply directly to your business, I've included them to serve as a stimulus so you can begin thinking of what you might consider applying in your business that can help you develop trust and loyalty with your customers.

In our coaching programs, we go into great detail, and discuss more than two-dozen very specific strategies that create an almost magnetic effect, that keeps your customers returning time and time again.

We lead you by the hand and help you develop personalized and effective strategies that keep them saying, "I'll be back"... strategies that keep them "insulated" from, and locked out of your competition.

Now let's talk about the fourth method you can use to grow your business. And that is, to…

Extend Your Customers' "Average Buying Lifetime"

We call that, "Customer Retention."

Here's what I mean: How long, on average, do the people who buy from you, your customers, remain your customers?

In other words, how long do they continue doing business with you before they move on? Are they one-time buyers? Do they stay with you for a year, five years or ten years? Have you ever stopped to figure it out? This is an important step, and one that we'll be discussing in more detail in later pages.

Next, what are you doing in your business *right now*, to make sure your customers *continue* doing business with you? If you don't have a strategic plan, a *working system* in place, you are going to lose a certain percent of your current customers to the competition.

There's no question about it. Your competition… *right now*… *right this very minute*, is making plans and taking steps to take your customers away from you.

The question for you, is not, "What are you going to do about it?"

The *real* question is, "What are you *currently* doing about it?"

"What are you doing about it *right no*w?"

What plans... what *systems* do you have in place to keep your customers from defecting to the competition?

Let's talk about your customers for a minute. Are they *thrilled* enough with the products you offer and the services they receive from you to continue doing business with you year after year?

What if you answered "yes" to that question?

My next questions would be, "Are you sure?"

"How do you know?"

"Where did you get your information?"

"How reliable is it?"

"Can you explain in, detail, the *system* you have in place for finding out?"

Notice that I said, "Are they *thrilled* enough?" Not "are they *satisfied* enough?" You see, there's a big difference between being *thrilled* and being *satisfie*d.

Last year, more than 200 million Americans stopped doing business with companies that they were "satisfied" with. And sixty percent of so-called "satisfied" customers switch companies or brands on a regular basis.

As a business owner, you can't afford not to thrill your customers, nor to build trust in you and your business. The cost is too high, and unfortunately, most business owners simply don't understand it. Let's take a look at what the potential cost could be to you if you fail to do these things:

Let's say that you make $200 in sales per year from your average customer.

And let's say that for any number of reasons, 100 customers stop doing business with you each year. They may die or move away. They may no longer have need for your products or services, they may switch companies, have a relative in the business, or possibly have a bad experience with someone in your company.

Or, they may just simply disagree with some policy or procedure you might have. It could be a falling out with a staff member or employee, a personality conflict, miscommunication, a problem they had with one of your products, or perhaps a feeling of neglect from you or someone in your business. It really doesn't matter what the reason, they just stop doing business with you.

Well, those 100 customers no longer paying you $200 this year just cost you $20,000. But, that's not all. What if those 100 customers tell 5 others about their experience with you?

That's an additional 500 potential customers who won't be doing business with you this year (or maybe ever, for that matter).

And if each of them spent an average of $200, that's $100,000 you won't be receiving from them, *PLUS* the $20,000 you lost on your existing customers who left.

That brings the total in lost income to *$120,000 in just one year!*

It's not unusual for some businesses to bring in a hundred (or more) new customers each month. That's twelve hundred-plus, customers a year. And they end up only netting a 150 or 200 increase at year-end (sometimes not even that).

Well, what happened to the other more than 1,000 customers? Where did they go? Surely, they all didn't die, or move away.

But, you know, most business owners don't concern themselves with what, or whom they've lost. They just focus on their net gain. They figure that if they finish the year with more customers or more sales than they started with, they're ahead.

Now, let's suppose that you gave those 100 lost customers reasons... good, compelling, life or business enhancing reasons to continue doing business with you this year.

And let's suppose each of them told those same five people about their now-positive experience with you.

Well, there's $20,000 you wouldn't have lost in the first place, and another $100,000 you may possibly pick up from their referrals or by their word of mouth.

The point is, customers are important – *all* customers. In fact, they're critical. There's no question about it. You and I both know that. A business couldn't remain in business, unless it has someone to buy its products and services.

Those "someone's" are people. Real people. People like you and like me. If you sell your products to the business community, remember, businesses don't buy from businesses.

People in business buy from other people in business. It's people that you market to. Not businesses.

Here's an interesting point: Most business owners know exactly how much they have tied up in furniture, fixtures and equipment. They can tell you, nearly to the penny, how much each item costs, how old it is, how much it's depreciated and what the remaining life expectancy is.

That's important information for any business to have. There's no question about it. But what's amazing is that very few business owners have any idea of what the value of their most important asset is... their customers.

Think about how this whole concept relates to your business, for a minute. What is it that you can do, *specifically*, to extend your customer's buying lifetime with you? Why not take a few minutes and answer these questions?

First of all, who are your customers ... those who are buying from you now?

Who are their family members?

Do you know the names and ages of their spouse or children?

Do you know where they work?

What about their spouse or children?

What are their hobbies or interests?

Do you know why they purchased a certain type of product or service?

Do you know who their friends, neighbors or relatives are?

What about your staff or employees? Do you know how they treat or feel about your customers?

Do they, or do you, for that matter, have *favorite* customers? What makes them a "favorite?" Is it how much they spend? How often they come in? Their personality? And how do you treat those customers? Any different than the others?

Do you have regular staff meetings and talk about how to think like a customer?

What you would want if you were a prospect considering doing business with you for the first time? Or maybe an existing customers considering giving repeat business to your establishment or organization?

Or, perhaps considering referring a friend, a family member or an acquaintance?

Do you have a training system in place to teach your staff how to handle or deal with difficult customers? Short-tempered customers? Analytical customers?

Do you have a plan for moving people up the Loyalty Ladder? From Suspect to Prospect to Shopper. Then on to Customer, Client, and Advocate. And, finally to convert them into Raving Fans?

When a customer stops doing business with you, do you know why? Do you have a *system* in place to find out?

What would you have to do differently to get your customers to buy from you for, say, 5 ½ years, instead of just 5 years?

Believe me, if you will actually take the time to go through these questions and formulate answers for them, and then incorporate that information into your business practices, you can work wonders towards extending the buying lifetime of your customers. And as a result, you'll add *significant* profits to your bottom line.

We've covered a lot of ground and a lot of ideas, so far. So, let's pause for a minute, and recap what we've discussed up to this point. There are four primary ways to grow a business.

First, **get more customers**. And as I mentioned, this is a vital step. But it's also the most difficult and the most costly.

Second, is **get your customers to spend more money with you...** increase the average transactional value of each sale. And remember, that this is the fastest and the easiest way to add immediate profits to your bottom line.

Third, **get your customers coming back to buy from you more often.**

And, fourth, **extend your customers' buying lifetime**. Find ways to retain them, keep them as customers and keep them coming back as long as you possibly can. It's really pretty simple. Nearly everything you do to build and grow your business can be slotted under one of these four categories. As I mentioned earlier, there are more than two-dozen ways to apply these concepts and build your business, but for now, if you'll work on these four primary methods, you'll absolutely run circles around your competitors.

As you take a good, close-up look at these four areas, you'll see that what it really boils down to, is effectively marketing your business to your customers and potential customers.

In other words, the success of your business enterprise depends, largely, on how effective your marketing system is.

And that means that if you want your business to excel... to really excel... if you want to virtually eliminate your competition, and become the dominating force in your marketplace, then you've got to begin thinking of yourself as being in the *marketing* business, not in the product or service selling business.

In effect, you need to consider yourself as the head of a marketing organization that sells the products and services that your business offers.

Once you begin operating effectively at that point, you'll find that your job becomes much easier and much more enjoyable, and your prospects and customers will begin seeking you out and referring others to you, rather than you chasing after them. The net result will be that your marketing costs will plummet, and your profits will skyrocket!

7

How Much Are Your Customers Really Worth?

Determining the Lifetime Profit Value of Your Customers

"Only a life lived for others is a life worthwhile."

– Albert Einstein

There's not much debate about this fact: Your existing customers or clients are your most valuable assets. The question is, how much are they worth?

How much money... how much *profit* will you realize from each of your customers, over their "buying lifetime" with you?

This is such an important concept, and I can't say it strongly enough, that just knowing and understanding this one thing, can have a bigger impact on your business than just about anything else you can do.

Once you understand it, a whole new set of factors will come into play, and can absolutely revolutionize the way you look at your business, the way you *do* business, and the profits you'll generate as a result. Let me give you an example to explain what I mean.

Let's say that your average sale is $50. And let's say that your average customer buys from you 4 times per year.

So from those four transactions, you realize $200 in income. And let's say that this customer does business with you on average, for 10 years. Over that 10-year period (or their "lifetime" of doing business with you), that average customer has been worth $2,000 in income to you.

Now, let's expand this example to a theoretical base of 1,000 customers and see what it means. Those 1,000 customers at $200 a year nets you an annual income of $200,000.

Let's assume that with the proper programs in place that you're able to increase each of the 4 ways to grow your business that we discussed earlier, by only 10 percent. Here's what happens:

First, the number of customers you have, increases from 1,000 to 1,100.

Next, the average transaction amount per sale increases from $50 to $55.

Third, the average number of purchases per customer increases from 4 times 4.4 times.

So, the annual income from your customer base will increase from $200,000 ($50 x 4 transactions x 1,000 customers) to $266,200 ($55 x 4.4 x 1,100 customers). That's an increase of $66,200 a year!

That's a huge increase! But if you think that's exciting, wait till you see what happens if you were to extend your customer's buying lifetime by just 10 percent.

Let's say that your customers stay with you for 10 years, on average. Your lifetime value from those customers over that period of time would normally be $2,000,000. But, if you can extend that 10 years by just 10 percent to 11 years, your total dollar value from these customers will increase from $2,000,000 to $2,928,200 ($266,200 x 11 years)!

An increase of $928,200... nearly a million dollars! That's a *major* increase!

But that's not all. Let's say that you put an effective referral generating system in place, and that just 10 percent of your 1,000 customers sends you a referral with a buying profile the same as your average customer.

That's an additional 100 customers who will bring you income of another $266,200 over the 11 years ($55 x 4.4 renewals x 100 customers x 11 years).

Total it all up, and you just made an additional $1,194,400! That's an average of $1,085,818 per year over the 11 years! Sound impossible? Well, it's not. And it's not all that difficult, either. It can be done by simply increasing each of the four areas by only 10 percent!

Now, how hard would that be to do in your business? Could you realistically, and with some help, increase each of the four areas we discussed, by ten percent? What about twenty percent?

Some businesses after realizing the power of this key concept, and the others that we've discussed, have increased their businesses by as much as a hundred percent or more in less than a year.

Maybe the numbers and figures I've discussed are realistic for you and your business, and maybe they're not. And maybe you can't increase each of the areas by the same percentage. That's okay. That doesn't matter.

The point is you probably have room for improvement in one, or more of the four areas. And if you want your business to be a viable force in the marketplace, and to give you the lifestyle, the satisfaction and the income you want, you're going to have to take some proactive steps.

Knowing the Value of Your Customers Influences the Way You Treat Them

As I mentioned before, just knowing how much your customers are worth to you can be invaluable, and can help you in several ways.

First of all, we know that people don't do business with the same company or business forever. They stop doing business or change whom they do business with for a variety of reasons, and we've already discussed some of those.

But, if you just know, for instance, that your typical customer stays with you for say, ten years, on average, that they're not just a one or two-time sale, you may begin to treat them differently.

You may treat them with more respect, more kindness, and more courtesy. You may give them some form of special treatment. And you may even invite them to special, invitation-only, preferred customer seminars or events.

In other words, once you begin to see your customers in a different light, you may begin to do things differently in order to get them to stay longer as customers.

Next, if you know what the Lifetime Profit Value of your customers is, you'll probably discover that you can spend far more to acquire a new customer than you originally thought.

In other words, if your average customer is worth $2,000 in income to you, you can, theoretically, afford to spend up to $2,000 to bring in a new customer and still break even.

In theory, you could spend that $2,000 and still make a profit on the other "back end" products that you might be able to sell them.

And, if you put an effective referral-generating program in place, you can spend that same $2,000, and make your profits on the referrals they generate.

You and I both know that it's unrealistic to think that you can really afford to spend the full amount of your lifetime income (in this case, $2,000), to get each new customer. And I'm certainly not suggesting that.

In reality, you *can't* spend the entire $2,000. You've got to be concerned about things like overhead, cash-flow and reserves. You can't spend money you don't have.

And, you have to make sure that the customers you attract, at least match the profile of your average customers, or perhaps are even a little better than average.

There are a number of other things that you need to be aware of, as well, such as, "Cost of Acquisition," "Cost of Retention," understanding your margins, and calculating the Marginal Net Worth of your customers. Unfortunately, we don't have time to cover them in sufficient detail, here.

Knowing the Value of Your Customers Influences How Much You Can Spend To Get a New One, or Keep an Existing One

What it really comes down to, are two questions: How much can you *afford* to spend, and how much are you *willing* to spend to attract new business?

You may find that you can, and are willing to spend five or six times what your competitors spend. And if they're not willing to keep up with you, your business may just explode and leave them in the dust.

Just knowing what your *margins* are, and that you could, if you had to, spend up to that $2,000 amount and still break even, gives you a *tremendous* edge over your competition.

Here's a real-life example: I have a favorite restaurant I like to go to about twice a month. My meals typically come to about $30. So $30 times 24 meals adds up to $720 in gross sales for the year.

Let's suppose that I continue to patronize that restaurant for, say, 10 years. That's my buying lifetime with that particular restaurant. That gives the restaurant a total of $7,200 in sales.

If over that 10-year period, I refer 10 people, 5 of whom become regular customers (and that's not very many in 10 years), who have spending patterns similar to mine, they'll spend an additional $36,000. (That's 5 people, times $7,200 a year.)

Add that to the $7,200 that I spent, and I've been responsible for generating $43,200 for that restaurant. Even after deducting expenses for overhead, salaries and food costs, the restaurant still realizes a pretty substantial number of profit dollars from the efforts of just one person.

Restaurant Example	
A. Amount of average sale	$ 30
B. No. of sales/year/customer (2 x per month)	24
C. Gross income per year per customer (A x B)	$720
D. No. of years customer patronizes restaurant	10
E. Gross income over buying lifetime (C x D)	$7,200
F. No. of referrals from customer over buying lifetime	10
G. % of referrals who become a customer	50%
H. Referrals who become customers (D x E)	5
I. Gross income from referrals (E x H)	$6,000
J. Total value of a loyal customer (E + I)	$13,200

Now, here's a question: Could that restaurant afford to give away a free meal to attract a new customer? Keep in mind that I am spending $30, and out of that, about a third of it (or, maybe $10) is profit.

So, the meal really only costs the restaurant $10 for the meal, and only part of that $10 goes to cover the cost of the food.

The rest of the expense is in overhead, which would have to be paid whether or not a meal was served.

Well, of course the answer is yes, they *can* afford to give away a free meal. Not only that, but they can afford to do a number of other things to not only attract new customers, but more important, make their existing customers feel more appreciated and more special. And you know, when someone feels noticed and important, appreciated and special, it's just natural that they'll want to return.

Let's imagine, for a minute, that you are a long-time, faithful customer of a certain restaurant. And you brought your family, your clients or your business associates with you to eat there on a regular basis.

How would *you* feel, if sometime, the manager of the restaurant were to offer you and your party a free dessert as a special appreciation gift for your loyalty and for the extra business you brought them? Do you think that little display of appreciation would cause you to want to return again? I think it's pretty safe to say that it probably would.

And what about the people who were with you? How do you think they would feel? Do you think they would want to go back to that restaurant? Sure they would. What do you think the restaurant's hard costs of those desserts would be? Do you think the restaurant would lose any money on that gesture?

Well, it's not likely. You see, once you know how much profit your customers are worth to you, long term, then, and only then, can you determine how much you can afford to give away, or to spend, to get new customers, or to keep your existing customers coming back. And you can begin to experiment with different offers to see which ones work best.

Now, here's another thought. Let's say that the owner of that restaurant runs an ad, or does a mailing to attract new customers.

And let's say he spends $1,000 for the ad or the mailing, and two couples come in for dinner, and each spends $30.

Well, he's taken in a total of $60. But the ad costs were $1,000. So what does he do? What would his competition do?

Does he consider the ad or mail campaign a loser...a total bust...and stop running it? That's what most business people do.

But what about you? What would you do? Well, if you understand the concept of Lifetime Profit Value and Marginal Net Worth, you'll probably think differently.

When you consider the Lifetime Value of those customers and realize that with the proper care and attention those customers could be responsible for $43,200 each, or $86,400 for the two of them, it changes the picture.

Of course, those numbers are gross revenue figures, and you have to deduct for expenses. And it's over a 10-year period. But, still, that represents a significant amount of money. And all from a $1,000 ad. An ad that most business owners would have given up on.

Now, I'm not saying that you have to settle for, and be happy with low response rates for your ads. Certainly, you don't. You should always try to improve your ads, your letters, your offers... and give good, compelling reasons and benefits for someone to do business with you.

That's an entire subject, itself, and one we don't have time to discuss in great detail here. But one we take very seriously, and spend considerable time on in our workshops and coaching programs.

Let's go back and think about our restaurant example for a minute. Did this idea of stopping an ad just because it didn't break even, or produce a profit for you sound unusual? Different? Strange? Well, maybe to some people, in some businesses.

But, supermarkets and department stores use their own adaptation of this technique all the time. You've probably heard it referred to as a "loss leader."

What they do, is advertise a few products at, or below cost to bring new customers in to their store, knowing that the customer will usually buy more products once they're in the store.

And also knowing, that unless they get someone to visit their store in the first place, they could never stand a chance of making additional or repeat sales, or getting referrals from them. And additional and repeat sales to existing customers are generally easier to make, and usually always bring higher profit margins.

Just remember this important point:

The first sale means nothing... unless you're planning on going out of business next week.

You've got to consider the Lifetime Profit Value...what your customer is worth to you...if you really want to be successful.

Now, what about you, in your business? How can you apply this concept of Lifetime Profit Value?

Well, the first thing you can do is determine what the amount of your average income per sale is. The Lifetime Profit Value Calculator below is provided for you to use in calculating the Lifetime Profit Value of your own customers. Fill out with your current figures to get an idea of how much your customers are worth to you.

The LPV of Your Customers (Actual)	
A. Amount of average sale	$
B. No. of sales/year/customer (2 x per month)	
C. Gross income per year per customer (A x B)	$
D. No. of years customer patronizes restaurant	
E. Gross income over buying lifetime (C x D)	$
F. No. of referrals from customer over buying lifetime	
G. % of referrals who become a customer	%
H. Referrals who become customers (D x E)	
I. Gross income from referrals (E x H)	$
J. Total value of a loyal customer (E + I)	$

The calculator on the following page is provided so you can calculate what kind of a difference it will make to your business if you increased each of the areas by 10 percent.

Keep in mind as you do these calculations, that this is a very simplified calculation. In our consulting sessions we get very detailed and take into consideration many more areas. So the results you'll see in actuality will be dramatically increased. But for a simple and easy to demonstrate way to determine your customers' value to you, these basic calculators will do quite nicely.

The LPV of Your Customers (+10%)	
A. Amount of average sale	$
B. No. of sales/year/customer (2 x per month)	
C. Gross income per year per customer (A x B)	$
D. No. of years customer patronizes restaurant	
E. Gross income over buying lifetime (C x D)	$
F. No. of referrals from customer over buying lifetime	
G. % of referrals who become a customer	%
H. Referrals who become customers (D x E)	
I. Gross income from referrals (E x H)	$
J. Total value of a loyal customer (E + I)	$

Epilogue

Where Do You Go From Here?

Congratulations for making it this far. You have now been exposed to some of the most powerful and effective techniques, concepts and ideas available for succeeding in business.

But no matter how good these ideas are, just being exposed to them is not enough. You must also do something with them. In order for you to get the most value out of this material, you might want to consider developing a step-by-step action plan. An effective and results producing plan should consist of 5 areas:

1. EVALUATION

Ideas are nothing more than ideas until they are put into action. Once acted on, they have the potential to literally turn around a struggling business, or help an already successful business become even more dynamic and successful.

But before a person runs out and implements a new-found idea, they should first take the time to evaluate their operation to determine just what areas are most lacking and could use the most attention.

You have the potential of making the most improvement in your own business, if you will take the time to identify and work on the area of greatest need, first.

2. RESEARCH

Once you've identified your greatest needs and placed them in priority order, you can begin to search out available solutions. Be on an opportunity lookout. The material in this book is just the beginning of the many places you can find good, usable, and practical ideas.

Don't turn any ideas away just because you think they might not pertain to your business or the way you operate. Capture them and then apply step number three.

3. PERSONALIZATION

As you encounter new ideas, keep an open mind. Study them. Analyze them. And think them through. Ask yourself if an application can be made to your specific situation by simply changing or modifying part of the concept or idea.

If a certain illustration uses a certain type of product or service for the example, but you don't sell that product or service, a simple adjustment might be all that's needed.

The material in the book is designed to illustrate concepts, and only uses certain types of products as examples to make various points.

4. IMPLEMENTATION

Just as a membership in a health club won't do its owner any good unless he or she goes to the club and participates in the exercise program, so too, with the information in this book.

It's of no practical use unless it is implemented. It's easy to come up with good ideas and develop plans, but where most people get bogged down is when it comes to putting them into action. It's not always easy, but if you're going to truly be successful, you must do whatever it takes to act on your plans.

5. REVIEW

After you've worked with your new ideas for a period of time, stop and evaluate how things are working. You may need to make some adjustments so you can continue to see improvement.

Sometimes, an idea you thought was great, doesn't work out at all. That's okay, don't continue using it. Just scrap it and move on to something else.

On the other hand, if you find an idea that works well, see if you can refine it, or make it even more effective.

That's all there is to it. Sounds simple enough to say, but in reality, there's a lot to do. The plain and truthful facts are, that most people simply won't take the time and effort to do the things we've just discussed. That's unfortunate on one hand, because they could be even more successful than they are now.

On the other hand, their failure to take action is good for you. Because if it's you that does these things and not them, it will be you who realizes the success.

Now you have the tools...

GO FOR IT!

About the Author

Greg Jones has been a successful entre-preneur, business builder, patented inventor and marketing professional for 28 years. His specialty and passion is developing marketing systems for small to mid-sized businesses and business start-ups with a focus on customer acquisition, customer retention and developing multiple profit centers for those businesses.

Greg's hobbies are reading, music and traveling.

He enjoys spending time with Beverly, his wife of 42 years, their two children and eight grand-children.

Greg is a gifted communicator and enjoys holding seminars and conferences related to dynamic business growth and innovative marketing systems.

He can be reached at:
velocitychainreaction@gmail.com